Exotic Species

Exotic Species

Invaders in Paradise

BRENDA Z. GUIBERSON

Twenty-First Century Books
Brookfield, Connecticut

For the honeycreepers, the burrowing owls,
and all those creatures living so close to the edge.

B. Z. G.

Cover photograph courtesy of Animals, Animals (© Stephen Dalton)

Photographs courtesy of Visuals Unlimited: pp. 11 (© Charlie Heidecker), 20 (© Bill Beatty), 30 (© Ken Wagner), 71 (© Walt Anderson); Peter Arnold, Inc.: pp. 12 (© Carl R. Sams II), 16 (© John Cancalosi), 19 (© Manfred Danegger), 65 (© P. Aitken); © Boston Herald: p. 23; The National Audubon Society Collection/Photo Researchers: pp. 27 (© 1984 Angelina Lax), 29 (© 1987 Nancy J. Pierce), 33 (Holt Studios/Nigel Cattlin), 36 (Peter Yates/Science Photo Library), 57 (© John Mitchell), 69 (© S. J. Krasemann), 73 (©Klaus Guldbrandsen/Science Photo Library); Michigan Sea Grant: pp. 38, 41, 43; Animals, Animals: pp. 49 (© Phil Degginger), 50 (© 1987 Victoria McCormick), 60 (© David C. Fritts); Department of Land and Natural Resources: p. 52 (Linda McCrerey); Chris Johns/National Geographic Image Collection: pp. 54, 58

Library of Congress Cataloging-in-Publication Data
Guiberson, Brenda Z.
Exotic species: invaders in paradise / by Brenda Guiberson.
p.   cm.
Includes bibliographical references (p.   ) and index.
Summary: Examines the topic of species that have been introduced into a new environment and have subsequently harmed the established species. Included are starlings, zebra mussels, kudzu, and mountain goats.
ISBN 0-7613-1319-2 (lib. bdg.)
1. Biological invasions—Juvenile literature. 2. Animal introduction—Juvenile literature. 3. Alien plants—Juvenile literature. [1. Animal introduction. 2. Plant introduction.] I. Title.
QH353.G85   1999
577´.18—DC21   98-41508   CIP   AC

Published by Twenty-First Century Books
A Division of The Millbrook Press, Inc.
2 Old New Milford Road, Brookfield, Connecticut 06804

CONTENTS

Exotic Species

CHAPTER ONE

Nature's Great Balancing Act

P lants and animals that live together over hundreds or even thousands of years develop fascinating ways to share the same space. For instance, prairie dogs in the western United States dig tunnels into the earth and make great underground cities. One city found in Texas had about four hundred million animals. Other prairie creatures, like burrowing owls, snakes, and frogs, can't dig their own tunnels but find good shelter in abandoned prairie dog tunnels. Black-footed ferrets not only live in these same tunnels, but they catch prairie dogs for food. Hawks, coyotes, eagles, badgers, and many others also eat prairie dogs. Altogether, millions of prairie dogs in a huge, healthy, underground city can support at least 170 other types of animals.

Prairie dogs, however, are not popular with people. Some western states even consider the animals an official pest. Prairie dogs eat grass, and ranchers do not like to share grazing land meant for their cattle. Ranchers also fear their animals might step into a prairie dog hole and break a leg. Homeowners and farmers cringe when they see prairie dogs dig through their lawns or cropland.

In a battle over the grasslands, prairie dogs have been poisoned, shot, and bulldozed until 98 percent of them are gone. As a result, owls and ferrets that depended on them are very close to extinction. Hawks, foxes, and other animals that eat prairie dogs are declining in numbers, too.

Plants and animals make connections that allow one to survive because another survives. They create a great balancing act. Local life ticks together like a smoothly running clock. If one species gets out of balance—either too many or too few—other species will also be affected.

Sometimes a relationship develops between plants. A fungus, for instance, cannot make its own food. It grows on the roots of a tree and uses food that the tree can make. In return, the fungus draws in extra water and nitrogen for the tree. A tree cannot thrive without the fungus and the fungus cannot eat without the tree. Another connection in this relationship involves the flying squirrel. The squirrel eats the fruit of the fungus. Then as it scampers around the forest, it spreads the fungus to new trees in its droppings. Guess who lives in these thriving trees? The flying squirrel— which is eaten by owls that also live in the trees in this same community.

Sometimes plants develop special relationships with the creatures that help them to reproduce by pollination. Bees and butterflies spread pollen around in the daytime, when they get their food from blossoms. The evening primrose blooms at night. How does the plant survive? The night hawk moth, a rare night insect, comes out to eat from the primrose and carry its pollen from plant to plant in the darkness. Each type of fig tree has a single species of wasp that lives in it and provides pollination. The fig wasps need about three hundred trees as a food source to sustain a population. In Hawaii, birds called honeycreepers are pollinators. Some have developed long, curved beaks that allow them to reach the nectar in long, curved plant blossoms. If there is no pollinator, the plant cannot reproduce; if there is no plant, the pollinator will go hungry.

A burrowing owl defends its nest site. These birds often nest in abandoned tunnels dug by prairie dogs.

The night hawk moth is essential to the survival of the evening primrose.

Insects sometimes develop connections with other insects. Ants, for instance, raise aphids almost like a rancher raises a herd of cattle. When the aphids "overgraze" an area, the ants carry them to new "pastures." The aphids make a sweet liquid from the plants called honeydew. This honeydew drips from their bodies, and the ants "milk" it for their food. As the insects thrive, they become food for other creatures—keeping everything in balance.

These complex relationships have been developing for thousands, even millions, of years in habitats all over the world. During freezing winters, arctic foxes follow huge polar bears across the ice to eat leftover bits of seals that the bears catch. When the foxes shed their winter coats, birds arriving to lay their eggs pick up this fur to line their nests. In Africa, oxpecker birds eat ticks off the bodies of giraffes, getting their meals while the giraffes get rid of irritating pests. In the ocean, fish perform the same parasite-removal service for turtles and other sea creatures.

ADJUST
OR DIE

Whenever an environment changes, creatures must adjust. For example, if a volcanic eruption covers a section of an island with dark lava, white moths in the area suddenly become very conspicuous. They are more easily seen and more quickly eaten. Soon the area has a greater abundance of dark moths—moths that are harder to see against the new dark background. Eventually a bird with better eyesight or other characteristics may have more success at catching the dark moths and will raise extra chicks because of its increased food supply. As the successful birds increase in numbers, the dark moths will decrease.

Creatures develop many defenses to help them survive. Birds that live in areas with meat-eating creatures on the ground build their nests up high. If there are no trees, some birds can balance on narrow rocky cliffs and lay uneven eggs that will not roll off. Plants protect themselves from grazing animals by developing thorns, prickles, foul odors, and nasty tastes. Insects have hard shells or stinging bites. Frogs and snakes make poison.

Because any defense requires a lot of energy, creatures develop just enough to survive the conditions around them and nothing more. If birds live on an island with no predators they may eventually lose the ability to fly. For those birds, flying would be a waste of energy.

When the great balancing act hums along in good order, nature performs many services for the earth. Trees provide flood and erosion control. Worms, prairie dogs, and dead plants renew the soil. Insects pollinate farm crops, birds scatter seeds, and wetlands keep the water clean. But there are many situations that can interrupt the balance. One of the biggest problems today is the invasion of exotic species.

STRANGERS IN
A NEW LAND

What is an exotic species? It can be a plant, animal, or even a disease that has traveled far to reach a new home. It might be big like a four-hundred-pound pig, or small like a mosquito. It could be brought in on purpose or totally by accident. Perhaps it has traveled thousands of miles on a ship or plane only to find itself in a place where it doesn't fit in. A parrot escaping from a bird cage in Minnesota will find the climate too chilly. A bark beetle that eats only tree insects will starve if it arrives at a desert without trees. A seed traveling on the muddy boots of a hiker may fall onto dry concrete and never sprout. Even if the traveler survives for a time, it must find a mate, a pollinator—whatever it needs to reproduce and become established. Usually this doesn't happen, and the alien or exotic species disappears unnoticed in the strange environment.

But on rare occasions, an exotic species arrives to find conditions that are even better than at home. The climate is right, the food is perfect, and best of all, there are no diseases, predators, or defenses in the area to keep it in check. This is an invader in paradise, able to thrive without any system of checks and balances to stop its spread. Reproducing rapidly, it can eliminate native species one after another because they don't have enough time to develop defenses against it. Great success for an exotic species is like throwing a wrench into smoothly running clockworks. Clunk! The local plants and animals, some of them not found anywhere else in the world, can be lost forever.

TRAVELERS PICK UP
THE PACE

Plants and animals have always moved from place to place, floating in the wind, drifting with ocean currents, traveling on migrating birds, or across a temporary ice bridge. But until humans set out to explore the world, exotic species never moved very far, and certainly not very often. In the last hundred years, however, these alien invaders have had incredible opportunities to travel. Often without knowing it, millions of people and their vehicles carry them. Snakes climb into the wheel wells of airplanes and go island hopping. Fruit flies lay tiny eggs in Georgia peaches and then get shipped off to a college student in Austria. Unusual fish and plants get dumped from aquariums. Ships load ballast water for stability on the ocean and then carry millions of teeming little water creatures to a new environment. The Suez Canal, the Panama Canal, and all the hundreds of water channels around the world are full of boats and barges providing new pathways for exotic species. Tourists and employees of global companies pack them into their luggage. Soldiers don't notice the stowaways on their vehicles when they get shipped from one remote island base to another.

MUSKRAT HEAVEN

In 1906, six muskrats from the United States were introduced into the Netherlands for the fur trade. The exotic muskrats had no predators there, loved the climate and the food, and started to reproduce. One pair of muskrats can produce fifty babies in a year. Would they be able to find enough places to live?

The Netherlands has numerous earthen dikes, carefully maintained since the Middle Ages to keep the lowland country from flooding. The muskrats saw these dikes as giant burrows, unlimited places to dig and make tunnels. With such an abundant habitat, the muskrats became invaders in paradise. In a few years there were millions of them building homes in the great system of dikes. Muskrats continue to tunnel and burrow and dig through the Netherlands and threaten to flood the whole country. Now the Dutch spend millions of dollars trying to maintain the dikes and control the rodents. Five hundred muskrat trappers were able to catch over

Introduced into the Netherlands in the early 1900s, muskrats are a costly nuisance and a threat to the nation's famous dikes.

three hundred thousand muskrats in 1996, but this was not enough and they are looking for other solutions.

The muskrats are just one story—six exotic invaders multiplying to millions to change the natural balance of a community. Another situation involves a beautiful black bird with "stars" in its feathers. The starling had an opposite journey, from Europe to the United States, and set up its first home right in the middle of a big city.

CHAPTER TWO

Starlings, Strong and Smart

hen Europeans first came to America, they were often homesick for the things they had left behind. Eugene Schieffelin missed the European birds. In the late 1800s, he decided to bring to his new homeland every bird mentioned by Shakespeare, the English playwright. He organized a bird society in New York State and soon imported the song thrush, the house sparrow, and others. In 1890, he sent for the European starling, a black bird with shimmering flashes of purple and green. In the autumn, the bird also had white spots that looked like "stars." Not knowing if the starlings would survive, he introduced about a hundred of them into Central Park in New York City.

The starlings fit right in and soon built their first nest under the eaves of the American Museum of Natural History. By 1898, they had adapted so well that populations were moving out in all directions. In 1929, one observer saw a flock estimated at ten thousand in Ontario, Canada. Others reported flocks of millions.

Nothing stopped the starlings, not even the height of the Rocky Mountains or the vastness of the Great Plains. The birds conquered all sorts of environments, and by 1969 there were two hundred million of them living all across the continent. The starlings were in paradise.

How could this alien bird establish itself so quickly, and over such a wide range? In the United States during the nineteenth century, the native birds were struggling to adapt to the changes brought by the new settlers. The birds were in a state of upheaval, quickly losing their habitat to new farms and cities. The starlings arrived with more experience at adapting. They had already spent thousands of years learning to live around huge numbers of people in Europe. They had better defenses and instincts to handle the changing environment.

ALIEN BIRDS
WITH SPECIAL STRENGTHS

Starlings are birds with many physical advantages. For instance, most birds that eat insects can only snap their beaks closed around a meal. Starlings, however, also have a strong muscle that lets them open their beaks with an equal force. With this muscle they can dig and pry up insects that other birds cannot get.

Starlings also have better vision than most birds. They can use each eye independently to see both far and close-up at the same moment. While other birds have to stop eating to check the landscape, starlings can eat without interruption—and get more food.

Starlings have other amazing feeding abilities. They can eat insects in trees like chickadees, snap up flying bugs like flycatchers and swallows, eat ticks off the backs of cattle like oxpeckers, munch livestock feed like cattle, gorge on garbage like gulls, and snack at fast-food restaurants like humans. If one food source is low, they can quickly switch to another. With all the dining possibilities available to them, they can often raise chicks twice a year, four eggs at a time.

Showing the white starlike spots it was named for, a starling perches on a branch.

Starlings are also stronger and more muscular than most birds. This allows them to push other birds right out of their nests. Starlings prefer to nest in a tree hole, but unlike woodpeckers, they are unable to make it themselves. A starling simply follows a woodpecker, waits until it excavates a nesting cavity, and then pushes the bird aside to take over the nest. Sometimes starlings will work in groups, like a gang, to get what they want. They will throw out eggs or chicks when they find a nest already occupied. A homeless starling will lay an egg in another bird's nest and let it raise the chick. Starlings will fight to the death just looking for a good place to sleep. They will also nest in mailboxes, hollow fenceposts, and chimneys.

Even so, with two hundred million birds and a decreasing number of trees, there is often a housing shortage. As starlings muscle their way into nesting spots, bluebirds, flickers, and other native birds suffer. To help the native birds out, some people are now making nesting houses for bluebirds with openings of 3.8 centimeters, too small for starlings to enter. They are also trying to replace nesting places for flickers and other woodpeckers. Eventually, some native birds may adapt by laying their eggs later in the season when the starlings are finished and no longer interested in evicting them from their nests.

No one knows exactly how smart starlings are, but they can do some amazing things. Shakespeare knew this when he wrote about teaching a starling to say, "Mortimer, Mortimer"—the name of an earl distrusted by King Henry IV—so the king's enemies could disturb the king's sleep. Mozart bought a starling in 1784 because it could whistle a line from a piano concerto he was composing.

A flock of starlings fills the sky as the sun rises over a suburban neighborhood.

Starlings have been heard to imitate fifty-six other bird species, including gulls, rails, and warblers. They can also mimic barking dogs, telephones, alarm clocks, and squeaking doors. They can imitate a cough, a sigh, and say "See you soon, baboon." One starling liked to chant "defense, defense" every time he watched a basketball game on TV!

One starling might seem clever, but large numbers of them can be annoying and destructive. They sometimes fly together in great flocks of thousands and tens of thousands, and are very noisy. One researcher counted 530 starlings in a cubic meter of cattails. With their droppings they ruin parks and picnic benches. They kill trees with too much fertilizer and create slippery sidewalks and dirty cars. A huge flock can eat an entire fruit crop and create a disastrous year for a farmer. In 1960, a large flock caused the crash of an airplane in Boston, killing 62 passengers and increasing the demand for starling control.

BATTLING THE BIRDS

People have experimented with many methods to get rid of these birds. They have tried firecrackers, cold showers from the fire department, a squadron of model airplanes, electric horns, thinned-out stands of trees, glue, and sacks of mothballs. They sprayed huge roosts with detergent to destroy the waterproofing in the birds' feathers. The wet birds started to shake and shiver, couldn't protect themselves from the cold, and died of hypothermia. A theater in Canada offered children free movie tickets if they brought in ten pairs of starling legs. A dairy farmer in New York killed starlings in his barn with poison but then dumped the carcasses in a field. Other birds and animals who fed on them died from the poison, too.

In the end, nothing has worked very well. Some efforts are more trouble than they are worth, others just drive the birds a few blocks down the street. To effectively reduce the population, it would be necessary to kill over 50 percent of the starlings. Most people have conceded defeat and are trying to find a way to live with the birds.

Flocks of starlings can clog airplane engines, sometimes with disastrous results, as in Boston in 1960.

WHAT GOOD ARE THEY?

Do people get any benefits from starlings? It would seem so, especially during the nesting season when starlings have great appetites. Starling parents return three hundred times a day to feed their chicks during a three-week growing period. They bring three or four bugs every trip. With all the starlings around and with two nestings each year, the young birds consume four trillion insects while they are growing up. Starlings help control insects, including clover weevils, grasshoppers, beetles, and others that can damage crops. In the Netherlands, where cutworms are a problem, birdhouses are being built for starlings. In a similar insect control program, 22.5 million starling nestboxes have been built in eastern Asia.

Despite this insect control benefit, starlings threaten the survival of native birds—birds that have played important roles for centuries. For instance, woodpeckers also eat insects and help to control the ones that could sicken or destroy a forest. As woodpeckers tap out nest cavities for themselves, they are also building homes that many other creatures will use. Perhaps even more importantly, scientists have studied the woodpecker's ability to endure constant jolts and pounding against the hard wood of trees. Based on the ability of a woodpecker's neck to withstand severe whiplash, scientists have designed a better crash helmet for humans. When a native species is lost to its community, it can also mean the loss of anything that we might learn from it in the future.

In 1900, after the starling invasion, the United States government passed the Lacy Act "whereby no birds or animals can be brought into the United States except under permit signed by the Secretary of Agriculture." This ban was a good beginning at controlling alien species, but it didn't include exotic plants, especially one that came to be known as "the green cancer" and "the scourge of the South."

CHAPTER THREE

Kudzu—the Vine They Love to Hate

L ocals say, "Don't sit still too long. It can grow a foot a day." Folk legends in Georgia warn people to close windows at night to keep "the green menace" out. Rumors call it the "mile a minute vine"—able to swallow up a house or even an inattentive cow. A poet describes these plants as "green, mindless, unkillable ghosts."

What is this plant that threatens the South? It is kudzu, an exotic vine that grows so well that some southerners assume the tale of Jack and the Beanstalk is about a boy careless with kudzu. It was first exhibited by Japan at the Philadelphia Exposition in 1876. From the very beginning, kudzu attracted attention. Visitors came by the Exposition daily to marvel at how fast kudzu could grow. It was beautiful, with purple flowers and a scent of grapes. A few people bought cuttings and planted the Asian vine to climb up over their front porches and shade them from the hot summer sun. What they didn't know—but would soon find out as kudzu grew rapidly in the warm, moist climate of the South—was that there were no predators or defenses here in America that would slow down its growth.

In 1902, Charles and Lillie Pleas of Florida discovered kudzu growing wild all over their backyard and were amazed. They said their animals "ate it like candy." They felt that kudzu—a type of plant called a legume, which can enrich soils—could also help the poor soils of the South by adding nitrogen. They promoted it everywhere and began to sell cuttings through the mail. It wasn't long before Mr. Pleas was investigated for mail fraud. Postal inspectors didn't believe kudzu could grow as fast as he claimed. Mr. Pleas gave them a demonstration, the case was dropped, and the mailings continued.

Then a railroad company started to give the vine away to encourage farmers to grow it. They hoped kudzu would be cut and dried into hay, which could then be hauled in their railroad cars. This would be very good for business. The government also got involved when it decided kudzu might be a way to restore the dry soil of the South that had been worn out by too much cotton, corn, and tobacco farming. The government actually paid people up to $8 an acre to plant it! Eventually eighty-five million seedlings were in the ground, and kudzu replaced cotton as the "king of the South."

During the 1940s, the exotic plant was very popular. A reporter wrote a book about the virtues of growing kudzu and promoted it on his radio show. He started the Kudzu Club of America and soon had over twenty thousand members. A Kudzu Queen was chosen in Auburn, Alabama. People hoped to make an easy living while feeding animals, preventing erosion, and restoring overused farmland at the same time.

A kudzu vine in bloom is a pretty sight, giving no indication of what a nuisance it can be.

THE INVADER
STARTS TO SPREAD

But some people who planted the Asian vine began to notice strange things. An Arkansas farmer warned: "When you plant kudzu, drop it and run!" Others watched nervously as kudzu raced into nearby fields and choked out fruit and nut trees and other crops. Wherever kudzu grew, other plants could not survive. When farmers tried to harvest it as a hay, the twisting mess of vines made cutting almost impossible. Kudzu was beginning to look like a major pest, choking out native plants and providing unwanted hiding places for green snakes.

With help from so many people, kudzu easily became an invader in paradise. The plant has a super root system that helps it to maintain this position. As vines spread out in all directions, every leaf node that touches the ground becomes a new plant. Each of these plants grows deep roots able to reach water unavailable to other plants. Farmers have dug up roots 20 feet deep and weighing hundreds of pounds! If they don't get the entire root, the plant grows back. Farmers can't burn kudzu with much success. While the plant can be burned at the surface, its roots can sit dormant for up to ten years and then grow again.

Kudzu is now flourishing beyond anyone's wildest dreams as it drapes across seven million acres of the American South. The thick, tangled vines cling and climb over everything in their path and then droop and billow, creating the look of a fantasy land. They can bury a car in a few weeks, smother a house over a summer, and cause trains to slip and stall as the vines creep over railroad tracks. Vines shoot up telephone poles and ruin transformers. They cover up road signs and cause accidents. They can even climb trees a hundred feet tall and then smother and destroy entire forests!

Thousands of people with jobs in power companies, railroads, and traffic departments battle with kudzu every day. Some say that the South is fighting another war and losing. It costs these businesses $20 million annually just to keep up.

Creeping kudzu will soon completely cover these cars in a South Carolina junkyard.

GETTING RID OF THE PEST

Sometimes the best way to cut through kudzu is with a chain saw. It takes years of persistence to clear it from an area. Overgrazing with cattle can help, and three different chemicals, called herbicides, can sometimes kill it. But the chemicals can also harm other plants and animals in the area.

Kudzu was welcomed into this country as a plant that could grow anywhere and quickly without fertilizer, irrigation, or replanting. It sounded like a good thing—until people realized exactly what was going on. Finally, in 1972, kudzu was classified as a weed for those very same qualities: it could grow anywhere and quickly. It was a plant out of balance in a new environment.

These utility poles in Tennessee are draped in kudzu. The vines cause damage not only to the telephone lines, but to transformers, as well.

MAKING THE BEST
OF IT

Since kudzu seems to be here to stay, it is useful to take a look at the plant's good qualities. These are most easily seen in its natural Asian habitat, where it is quite well behaved. Asia's cooler climate helps to keep kudzu under control. There are also seventy or eighty insects that eat kudzu, including some that appear to eat nothing else. The red fruit bug, for instance, eats so many leaves, buds, and seeds that some kudzu plants are unable to reproduce. But because kudzu is related to peas and soybeans, it would not be wise to import these insect predators to the United States without thorough study. The insects might choose to eat soybeans or other farm crops instead of kudzu, and end up doing more harm than good.

In Asian countries, kudzu is often served for dinner because it is a nutritious food. In Japan, it is a key ingredient in sesame tofu and other dishes and teas. It is also part of a popular confection called kudzu-zakura, bean paste coated with jelled kudzu and served on a cherry leaf. In China, kudzu root is sold as a cheap candy, sliced and eaten raw. Kudzu also makes a fine cooking starch for soups and sauces and a crisp coating for fried foods. The roots can be cooked like potatoes, the leaves eaten like greens, and there is even a recipe for kudzu jelly. In Asia, kudzu has been eaten for centuries, and there is evidence that the huge kudzu root has saved Japan from starvation during periods of famine in its past.

Kudzu vines can also be woven into strong baskets and fabric. Kudzu kimonos are highly prized because of their strength and texture. It is also used for wall coverings, cushions, handbags, and ropes. Many of these food and woven products are now being made in the United States as well.

MAKING A MENACE INTO
A MEDICINE

Like many plants, kudzu is full of chemicals, and the most amazing use of this vine may be as a medicine. In Asian countries, kudzu has been used as a treatment for alcoholism and many other ailments for thousands of years. Researchers at Harvard Medical School in Massachusetts have tested ingredients from kudzu on Syrian hamsters, which have shown they will drink a lot of alcohol if given the opportunity in laboratory tests. Treated with kudzu chemicals, however, the hamsters lose interest and drink about 50 percent less alcohol than untreated hamsters. A study of three hundred cases in China revealed that 80 percent of people treated with kudzu extract for two to four weeks no longer craved alcohol. If testing continues with good results, this exotic species may become an important source of medicine used to treat a difficult problem in our society.

CAN KUDZU BE CONTROLLED?

With these potential uses in mind, is it possible to grow kudzu in the South without harming the rest of the environment? Right now careful studies are being made about the possibility of using biological controls. A biological control is a natural enemy, such as a predator, parasite, or disease, introduced to slow down an exotic species. Chemical controls, like pesticides, have often been used in the past, but chemicals are dangerous to everything around them, including humans, plants, animals, and the soil. Chemical solutions sometimes fail because exotic species can develop resistance to them and then bounce back with an even larger population. Biological controls can also cause harm, but if thoroughly studied and understood, they have the potential to restore the natural balance.

Researchers in North Carolina have discovered that the soybean looper caterpillar loves to eat kudzu, enough to make a dent in the supply. The scientists have come up with a very complicated plan to make sure that the caterpillar does not turn into a moth that will then eat its way through valuable soybean crops. First, they inject the caterpillar larvae with the eggs of a stingless wasp. The presence of the eggs gives the caterpillars a great appetite. Early tests have shown that the hungry caterpillars can eat

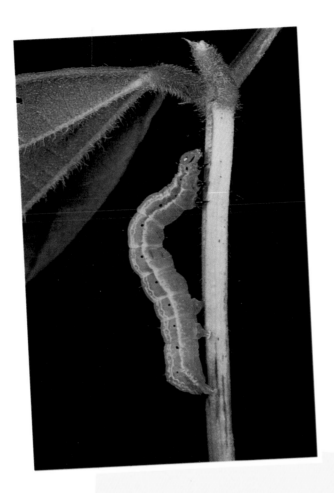

Soybean looper caterpillars seem to have an
enormous appetite for kudzu. Scientists are
hoping the caterpillar will turn out to be a way
of controlling the pesky vine.

enough kudzu leaves to kill the plants. Then, just in time to keep the caterpillar from turning into a moth, the wasp eggs perform their second job. They hatch before the caterpillar makes a cocoon and eat it up. Are the wasps then dangerous? The scientists have to check every possible consequence before considering putting a biological control into widespread use. Perhaps the soybean looper caterpillars will become the natural predator needed to keep kudzu in balance in the South.

Kudzu is also limited by climate. It likes the sun but will not grow in deserts, swamps, or places where its roots can be frozen deep underground. This means we needn't worry that kudzu will eventually take over the whole country!

This is the good news. The bad news is that another exotic species—"son of kudzu"—has invaded our shores. It is called Oriental bittersweet. This Asian native has been spotted from Tennessee to Virginia for about nine years, but no one is sure just how and where it first got established. Unlike kudzu, it can get started in a shady area, and cold weather does not keep it in check. This plant can weave itself into a mat 9 feet deep! Birds like to eat its bright berries, and then carry seeds to new areas in their droppings.

People are not helping to spread the "son of kudzu." Instead they are pulling the plant as soon as they find it in an effort to keep it in check. But sometimes an exotic species arrives that can hardly be seen. By the time we become aware of the danger, the invader may already be out of control.

CHAPTER FOUR

The Zebra Mussel Muscles In

In 1986 a ship prepares for a long journey from Europe to North America. Before departure, lake water is drawn up into the ship's hold to keep it stable during the rough Atlantic crossing. At the end of the journey, the ballast water is dumped into Lake St. Clair near Detroit. Like all water, it teems with microscopic creatures. Some of them are zebra mussels, floating in their tiny larval stage. They have just traveled thousands of miles to a new home. Will they be able to survive?

The zebra mussels are lucky. They came from fresh water and Lake St. Clair is fresh water, too. If they had been dumped into the ocean, the water would be too salty for them. But the zebra mussels are not like the lake's native clams and mussels. The natives are much bigger and burrow into the mud. Their larvae, called glochidia, move to new areas by hitching a ride on the local fish. The zebra mussels do not burrow. They are the only freshwater mussels to have a byssus, a clump of threads

A scientist from the United States Fish and Wildlife Service examines a cross section of a pipe clogged with zebra mussels. Infestations of these pests can shut down power plants and may threaten municipal water supply systems.

that allows them to clamp onto hard surfaces. The larvae are veligers, meaning they have tiny hairs that keep them floating in currents to find a new home. With these unusual behaviors, will they be able to thrive in this lake?

IN THE BEGINNING

The zebra mussels were first noticed by research scientists studying the lake bottom in 1988. They scooped up a rock that had a "wart" on it. After an investigation, they identified the wart: zebra mussel, dark and light stripes, typical adult about the size of a fingernail. They found about 240 of them per square yard of water, and they were concerned. The mussels had been causing problems in Europe for over a hundred years. In 1895 the decaying meat of dead zebra mussels shut down the water supply in Berlin for twenty-seven days. Sometimes they showed up in concentrations as high as 12,000 per square yard.

The scientists began a serious study. A short time later, they measured the density of zebra mussels in flowing water near a power plant and counted 1,200 of them per square yard. This was an alarming increase. Six months later, after the spawning season, they measured again and were astounded. The researchers discovered over nine hundred thousand zebra mussels per square yard, seventy-five times greater than the highest concentrations in Europe! The females were producing a million eggs at a time, and the zebra mussels were in paradise. The scientists could hardly imagine what effect this invasion would have on the environment of Lake St. Clair.

Clunk! The tiny zebra mussels started out by shutting down a power plant near Detroit. They clogged up the water pipes and filters. Since zebra mussels like to filter tiny plant life called phytoplankton from flowing water, they quickly attached themselves to the hard surfaces of the pipes where they could enjoy a constant picnic. The power plant closed

This supermarket cart, pulled up from underwater, is entirely encrusted with zebra mussels.

for repairs while scientists studied European solutions, such as wider, shorter pipes buried in sand, to fight the problem.

THE PROBLEM SPREADS

Meanwhile the zebra mussels traveled forty miles south into Lake Erie. In 1989, the twenty-two thousand citizens in Monroe, Michigan, noticed them when they clogged up their entire water supply. The fire fighting system shut down, schools were closed, the hospital cancelled surgeries, and people were told not to bathe or wash the dishes. Then boaters complained about the loss of a navigational buoy used to guide them safely through the lake. Divers investigated and found the buoy sunk under ten feet of water. It was weighed down with a huge colony of zebra mussels and no longer able to float.

While investigating a case in 1989, the police pulled up a car from the depths of Lake Erie. After just eight months under water, it was totally covered with a three-inch layer of zebra mussels. The mussels were attached to every available surface on this "mussel car"—glass, vinyl, rubber, metal, cloth, plastic, and fiberglass. Museums also discovered zebra mussels clinging to sunken ships and destroying the historical value of the shipwrecks.

Since no other creatures were competing for the hard surfaces, the zebra mussels used them all. They attached to boats, barges, trailers, ropes, anchors, shoes, birds—any hard surface that might carry them upstream, downstream, or over the land. The veligers followed the currents and canals. In just six years, zebra mussels moved into all the Great Lakes and eight river systems, including the Mississippi, Hudson, Ohio, Tennessee, and Illinois.

A NIGHTMARE
FOR NATIVES

This explosion of zebra mussels makes life impossible for many native mussel species. As native mussels stick their shells out of the mud to eat or reproduce, the zebra mussels use them for another hard surface. Some natives have been found with thousands of zebra mussels stacked on their shells! Under such a weight they suffocate and starve because they can't move, breathe, or open their shells to suck in water and filter out food. Sometimes a single zebra mussel clings to a tiny pebble, then other mussels cling to it and then to each other. Soon they form a great "mussel mat," as hard as concrete, that prevents the native mussels from burrowing into the mud. During a two-year study, eighteen species of native mussels disappeared and many others continue to be threatened.

The zebra mussels also anchor on the pitted limestone reefs where the local fish lay their eggs. This makes it difficult for fish called walleyes and other fish to spawn. As the zebra mussels eat, they filter incredible amounts of the tiny phytoplankton from the food chain. This leaves less food available for the fish and then less fish available for the birds and people that would eat them.

TINY MUSSELS—
BIG SURVIVORS

The zebra mussels have survival advantages everywhere. They can live for weeks in water sloshed onto a barge or into a fishing bucket as they get transported to a new area. They can starve for eleven months or clamp shut and live out of water for two weeks. In their tiny larval stage, when they are best seen with a microscope, they can hide anywhere. Sometimes they look and feel like tiny grains of sand on the bottom of a boat. Only an experienced observer would notice them in the cooling pipes of an engine. One of the few conditions that *will* stop zebra mussels is water that does not contain enough calcium for the larvae to make shells. They also cannot survive in water that is too hot or acidic.

People don't care to eat zebra mussels, or this would help keep the population in balance. One man who steamed up a bucket reported they smelled like a dead body and old gym socks. Only a few lake creatures have teeth and jaws strong enough to crack the zebra mussels' tiny shells. The scaup, a diving bird, and the drum, a fish, are able to eat them. The scaup have benefited from this new food source. In a two-year period, their population at Point Pelee National Park on Lake Erie increased from one hundred to twenty thousand birds. Even so, the thousands of birds are still not enough to make a dent in the zebra mussel population. Crayfish also eat these mussels, but zebra mussels often have the last word. Looking for more hard surfaces, they sometimes pile up on crayfish, covering their eyes and pincers and making it impossible for the crayfish to eat.

FIGHTING BACK

A proposal was made to import a black carp from Asia to eat the zebra mussels. This would be a method of biological control. However, no one could guarantee that the fish, which normally eats snails, would suddenly decide to eat only zebra mussels in its new environment. It might choose

Zebra mussels will attach themselves to any hard surface, whether it is living or dead.

instead to eat the endangered native mussels! And the carp might show up with a few exotic diseases or parasites. The native fish would have no resistance against them. Life for natives in the lake habitat would get worse, not better.

Utilities and power plants are constantly fighting the zebra mussels. Sometimes they blast them off with high pressure water hoses. At other times, they use chemicals like chlorine to kill them. But too much chlorine can also harm other life in the water. And millions of dead mussels create a new problem—a stinking mess that fouls up beaches. In Michigan, four methods are being tested to see if the dead mussels can't be made into fertilizer or other products. Utilities and industries estimate they will spend $5 billion in the next few years trying to keep ahead of this alien invader.

Zebra mussels are also a big problem for boaters. Mussels cling to the bottom of boats, slowing them down and causing them to use more fuel. If the mussels move up into the engine, they can make it overheat. It takes a lot of time and expense to keep a boat free from zebra mussels or to paint it with a special coating to repel the mussels. Boat owners really have no choice if they want to fight this exotic pest.

NAME ONE GOOD THING
ABOUT ZEBRA MUSSELS

Only a few positive uses have been discovered for zebra mussels. In the Netherlands they have been put into lakes to clean up algae growth. Each hungry little mussel can filter up to one liter of water a day. But there are more year-round diving birds and predatory fish in the Netherlands to keep the zebra mussel population in balance.

Zebra mussels are also useful because they are very sensitive to chemicals in the water around them. They will snap their shells closed when certain pollutants are present and they can stay closed for up to three

Education is the first step in the battle against zebra mussels. Posters like this one raise community awareness of the threat posed by these exotic invaders.

weeks without harm. Scientists have put tiny electrodes on some zebra mussels. The electrodes trigger an alarm system when the mussels snap shut. In this way, zebra mussels function as a warning device for water pollution.

In another experiment, zebra mussels have been put into bags in the water around a chemical plant. As the mussels filter out food, they also remove chemicals and are able to improve the water quality. However, as the water becomes less polluted, the mussels and the lake floor around them become more polluted and must be buried or burned as hazardous waste. Some birds that eat zebra mussels have been producing unhealthy eggs and this may be the result of getting extra pollutants from their food supply.

Another unusual effect involves divers working around the lakes and rivers where zebra mussels are found. Skilled divers are experiencing a multimillion-dollar growth in business as they find themselves in great demand to clean water filters, intake pipes, docks and buoys, over and over again.

A WIDESPREAD THREAT?

How far will these invading zebra mussels spread? Many thousands of boats travel through zebra mussel territory. Even if 99 percent of these boaters clean off their hulls before going to another area, just one boat getting through is enough to introduce this exotic species to a new home. In one six-month period, four boats hauled on trailers were found to be carrying unseen zebra mussels when inspected at the California border. It is probably only a matter of time before zebra mussels populate much of the fresh water in the United States. Meanwhile, scientists are experimenting with electrical fields, ultrasound, salt, and disruption of the mussels' reproductive cycle, trying to find a safe way to slow down the invasion.

Several areas have passed laws requiring boat owners to check their equipment. No one is allowed to motor up the St. Croix River that flows between Minnesota and Wisconsin without a special permit. The permit proves that the boat has been steam-cleaned or kept out of the water for seven dry days. Either method will kill the zebra mussels. Ships coming into the Great Lakes are asked to dump ballast water in the salty ocean before entering. Even the National Aeronautics and Space Administration has joined the fight against zebra mussels! NASA is helping to keep barges and tugboats larvae-free by checking far down into their pipes with a 25-foot video boroscope and rooting out the invaders hidden there. Hopefully these measures will help to check the spread of zebra mussels before more native mussels—mussels with such wonderful names as the orange-foot pimpleback, purple cat's paw, and southern pocketbook—disappear.

Zebra mussels are not the only reason native mussels have become extinct. In the last century, many have been affected by poor water quality, dams, and overharvesting. But anytime an exotic species successfully invades an area, the native species struggle to survive. This is especially apparent on islands, isolated places with numerous unique plants and animals that are found nowhere else on earth.

CHAPTER FIVE
The Hawaiian Islands— Paradise Lost

he Hawaiian islands were formed by volcanoes erupting under the sea millions of years ago. One after another, the islands popped up in the Pacific Ocean more than two thousand miles from the nearest continent. This is a very great, almost impossible distance for airborne seeds and drifting plants to travel. The islands were very isolated, and new species rarely managed to reach them except at the natural rate of once every fifty thousand years.

Only five families of land birds, probably blown in by great storms, found these remote islands. Some of the birds carried seeds, insects, and snails in their feathers, stomachs, or the mud on their feet. A few insects arrived in the air currents, and ferns drifted in as tiny spores. No ants, cockroaches, mosquitoes, amphibians, reptiles, or large forest trees ever got established. The only land mammal to reach Hawaii was a bat.

Because of this isolation, the life that managed to survive on Hawaii could move out into every little niche and evolve into thousands of new forms. The ferns and violets grew as big as trees. With no big animals around to eat or trample them, many birds and insects lost the ability to fly and lived right on the ground. Some snails grew without shells. Raspberries grew without thorns and mints without flavor, and other plants lost prickles, spines, poisons, nasty tastes, and foul odors, all unneeded defenses against grazing animals that were not there.

A single finch species evolved into fifty-four remarkable birds called honeycreepers. Some honeycreepers developed powerful beaks like pliers to crush twigs and eat the insects inside. Others had long, curved beaks to reach into long, thin flowers that seemed to grow just for them. Some had a tongue that worked like a straw to sip nectar. As the plants attracted specific birds and insects to their nectar, these creatures carried plant pollen from one blossom to another and became the pollinators. Everything fit together like a lock and key. Ninety-five percent of Hawaii's unique plants and animals could be found nowhere else on earth. The islands contributed a great number of unusual species to the variety of life on earth, including a bird that could eat like a land turtle.

CHANGE COMES
TO HAWAII

About fifteen hundred years ago, humans discovered the islands. They were the Polynesians who came in long canoes and brought many things with them from home, including dogs, chickens, small pigs (weighing about sixty pounds), and Polynesian rats. These exotic species, including the humans, were hungry and swarmed over the islands, grabbing up the eggs on the ground and catching flightless birds. The Polynesians also cut and burned lowland forests and planted bananas, sweet potatoes, and another root crop called taro. Sometimes they accidentally packed along a few weeds, like crabgrass, with the plants they brought from home. More and more exotic species arrived in the Hawaiian islands, and because the climate was so nice, many of them did very well. The success rate for new exotic species increased dramatically to three or four every hundred years. Native plants and birds, which had no defenses against these intruders, started to disappear.

The descendants of the Polynesians, the Hawaiians, took a further toll on native birds by collecting feathers to make capes, helmets, and ceremonial clothes. One chief, King Kamehameha the Great, had a beautiful yellow cape containing feathers from eighty thousand mamo birds. These black-bodied birds each had just a few yellow tail feathers.

Then the Europeans arrived. In 1778, Captain James Cook, an English navigator sent out to explore and map unknown parts of the world, discovered the islands. He left goats and large pigs behind as gifts. The pigs, some weighing up to 500 pounds, rooted up the soil to eat native plants and then wallowed in the mud to cool off. With these behaviors, they created new areas of loose, exposed soil—just the places for seeds of the new exotic plants to settle and get established. Then Captain George Vancouver, another English navigator, adding to Cook's explorations, introduced cattle and sheep, more grazing animals, to the Hawaiian islands. Missionaries and settlers followed with many new species. Rats escaped from ships or swam in from shipwrecks. As the islands filled up with exotic creatures, more native plants and birds became extinct.

At the end of the nineteenth century, fashionable people in the United States and Europe wanted bird feathers for their clothing and hats. To meet this demand, the bright native Hawaiian birds were heavily hunted. In one Hawaiian harbor, a Japanese ship was discovered with more than three hundred thousand dead birds in its hold. In 1909, just before leaving office, President Teddy Roosevelt created areas where birds could not be hunted in a desperate attempt to save some of the colorful birds.

Changes continued as farmers cut more native trees, like the ohia, to grow sugarcane, pineapple, and other crops. Many birds depended on the ohia for nectar. A new rat, the roof rat, arrived in the 1870s. The rats

The mongoose, introduced into Hawaii to help control a rat problem, feasted on native birds instead.

prospered quickly in the sugarcane fields and became a huge problem for the farmers. In the 1880s the farmers decided to try a method of biological control. They brought in mongooses from India to control the high rat population. Unfortunately they did not check carefully on mongoose behavior. The rats were active at night, but the mongoose hunted mostly in the daytime and rarely saw the rats. Instead, the mongooses often ate native birds, including the nene, a Hawaiian goose that does not fly well. As a result of the arrival of the mongoose, only a few hundred nene remain today.

The cat, horse, donkey, lizard, toad, axis deer, wallaby, cockroach, ant, rabbit, and many other exotic species were also brought to the islands. They ate native plants and left less and less food for the native birds. Or they ate the insects and birds that were the pollinators for the native plants. Without pollinators, native plants disappeared. Many native birds from Hawaii's past are now known to us only through a few skeletons they left behind.

The Hawaiian goose, or nene, is just one kind of native bird threatened by exotic species that have invaded Hawaii.

Some birds managed to hang on even into the 1890s. But in 1902, a scientist wrote that after hours in the woods, he did "not hear the note of a single native bird." He did not hear the "oo, amakihi, iiwi, akakani, omao, elepaio and others," some of the most wonderful songbirds found only in Hawaii.

THE MOSQUITO MENACE

Perhaps the final stress that became too much for some of the native bird species was the mosquito. In 1822, two missionaries wrote that one of the nicest things about the tropical islands was that "there are no mosquitoes here." But a few years later, a whaling ship traveling from Mexico stopped at a Hawaiian harbor. Sailors went ashore to fill a barrel with fresh drinking water. First, they dumped the last bit of stale water sloshing around in the barrel into the stream. Like most water, the water from the barrel was teeming with life. In this case it was the tiny larvae of a mosquito that transfers diseases from one bird to another.

Soon scientists began to notice "grievous afflictions"—lesions and tumors—on the faces, legs, and feet of many birds. The birds were getting bird pox and avian malaria. Without a defense against these diseases, they died quickly. The wild pigs, with their rooting, wallowing, and eating deep into the trunks of the ferns, created many new areas of pooled water where the mosquitoes could lay their eggs. The water troughs of cattle were also teeming with mosquito larvae.

Avian malaria is similar to human malaria. It is a parasite carried from victim to victim in mosquito saliva. The bird disease may have existed in infected exotic ducks and chickens in Hawaii for many years. The addition of the exotic mosquito was the factor that allowed the sickness to be carried to native birds.

Fortunately, the tropical mosquito could not survive in chilly places, and a few Hawaiian birds found refuge in the high volcanic mountains. They were no longer able, however, to continue pollinating native plants trying to survive in the lower elevations.

In the 1930s, regular airplane service started up in the islands. Over the next sixty years, invading species arrived almost continually, at more than a million times the natural rate and at twice the number absorbed each year in all of North America. The warm, mild climate helps many get a start. Hawaii even has its own version of kudzu called banana poka, a vine able to take over a forest and kill its trees.

HAWAII'S NATIVE
SPECIES NOW

Today, more than half of all the native bird species are extinct. Eight of those species were important as plant pollinators. Nearly half of the Hawaiian bird species remaining have such low numbers that they are en-

A ranger with the Hawaiian Forestry Service displays
banana poka vines at various stages in their growth.
Identifying exotic species correctly is essential before
attempting to control them.

dangered and close to becoming extinct. Hawaii's unique plants are also in trouble. Hundreds have become extinct, and 50 percent of those left are endangered. Three-fourths of all known extinctions in the United States are from Hawaii. One third of all endangered birds and plants belong to Hawaii, yet Hawaii has only 0.2 percent of the land mass.

California and other warm places that have far too many exotic species of their own are very concerned about the severe number of problems in the Hawaiian islands. They do not want any of the Hawaiian exotic species to travel to their area and get established. At a great loss to Hawaiian business, these places will not accept shipments from Hawaii that might contain a new exotic pest.

Hopefully, as people become more aware of what is being lost, changes can be made. One man who released pet rabbits into a national park was told about the Hawaiian island of Laysan. Pet rabbits brought to Laysan in 1903 had a population explosion that quickly turned the island into a desert and caused the extinction of the Laysan rail, millerbird, and honeycreeper. The man said he never would have released the pets if he understood the consequences of an exotic species eating its way through an environment where it does not belong.

People are working hard to save Hawaii's remaining native species. Some are looking for ways to protect the birds from disease. Others are creating areas free of rats and mongooses. A $2 million fence was built around Haleakala National Park to keep out wild goats and pigs. After just one year of protection, scientists saw grasses and native ferns sprouting back to life. The fence, however, is not able to keep out rats, rabbits, ants, or high-jumping axis deer, so these invaders are still causing considerable damage.

Because so many plants are disappearing, people are going to great lengths to find and save the last populations of native species. One plant, a type of lobelia, only survives on high sea cliffs, where wild pigs and goats cannot reach it. Mountain climbers have to dangle from these steep

Two botanists from the National Tropical Botanical Garden in Hawaii dangle from a cliff while collecting rare plants. Human intervention may be the only way to save some vanishing plant species.

places as they reach out with soft brushes to transfer pollen from one plant to another. The humans are the new pollinators, taking over this job from a moth that used to perform the service but is no longer seen. Another new pollinator is the Japanese white eye, a bird deliberately introduced into Hawaii in 1929. A rare success, this bird has been able to replace an extinct honeycreeper as the pollinator for a native plant called pandanus.

ON THE LOOKOUT
FOR THE
BROWN TREE SNAKE

Scientists are greatly concerned about letting any new exotic species get a start in Hawaii. Today, emergency response teams are set up around airports to spot invaders and to try to get rid of them before they can become established. Much of their efforts are focused on the brown tree snake, a recent invader in Guam, a nearby U.S. island territory with a military base. Because Hawaii also has a military base, anything that lives on Guam is likely to eventually reach Hawaii on a military ship or plane that travels between them. So far, the brown tree snake has been detected and stopped several times in Hawaii. If the snake ever got established there, the results could be the biggest horror story ever for the native species.

After World War II, brown tree snakes from the Solomon Islands managed to reach Guam, most likely on a military vehicle. The snakes came out only at night and at first no one really noticed them. When people did notice the snakes, they were incorrectly identified as Philippine rat snakes, which were not seen as a problem.

By 1980 the snakes were everywhere. They slithered into houses through toilet bowls and air conditioners. They bit people, injecting them with a mild venom that could poison small children and send them to the hospital. Every few days, a snake climbed up a power line and caused a power outage. Each blackout meant computer failures, lost business, and candlelight homework. Repairs became so frequent and expensive that the power company on Guam finally decided to shut off the power at night.

In the 1960s, people began to notice that the forests were strangely quiet. Where were the songbirds? Quickly the Guam flycatcher became extinct, followed by several other bird species. By the 1980s, nine of the eleven native songbird species on Guam had disappeared. The last few survivors were rescued by scientists and taken to places where the birds could be kept safe and perhaps rebuild their numbers.

The extinctions were a mystery. Researchers investigated pesticides, typhoons, and other possible causes. At this point, scientists finally got a correct identification on the exotic snake that had been causing so much trouble. It was a brown tree snake, a species that eats birds and their eggs. At first scientists were skeptical. How could a single snake species cause so many problems? The only other snake on the island was blind and very helpful—it ate termite and ant eggs.

Researchers performed a count and were astounded to find thirteen thousand brown tree snakes per square mile! Some were 8 feet long. As word got out about the scope and seriousness of the problem, officials in Hawaii knew they had to act to protect their remaining native birds from this snake. SWAT (Snake Watch and Alert Team) programs were set up in both Guam and Hawaii to check for snakes at the airports. Now dog patrols sniff through all the planes and luggage, but it is hard to keep track of military flights that do not have a schedule. Somehow these snakes have managed to reach six other Pacific Islands and even get to Corpus Cristi, Texas. Meanwhile, on Guam, people are using traps, poison, machetes, and dogs to try to get rid of the snakes. Electronic barriers have also been set up to protect bird nests, and scientists are breeding the last surviving birds and hoping to eventually return them to a place without snakes.

The brown tree snake turned out to be the culprit in a devastating ecological mystery on the island of Guam.

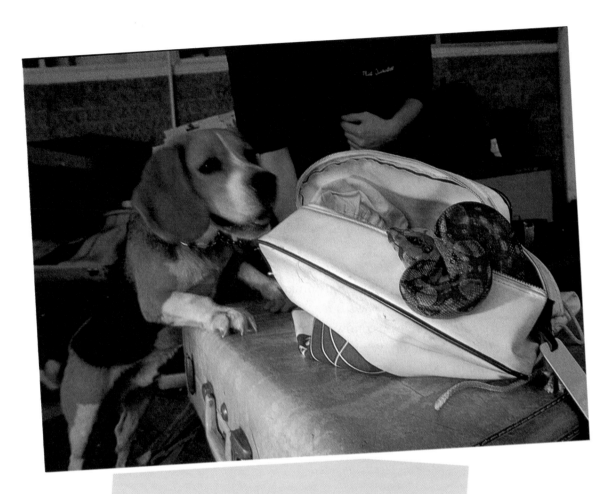

Snake-sniffing dogs check planes and
baggage at airports in both Hawaii and
Guam, searching for brown tree snakes.

LOOKING TOWARD THE FUTURE

Not long ago, a group of people in the Pacific islands of Micronesia decided to make and paddle great Polynesian canoes thousands of miles across the ocean to Hawaii in the old way, using only the water and stars to guide them. But even on this slow, hard trip, the sailors realized they were transporting something new to Hawaii. Little biting gnats from Micronesia were in their food and jumping around in the canoes. Surely residents and tourists of Hawaii would not appreciate these biting insects invading the beaches of the island paradise. Before they rowed into a Hawaiian harbor, the travellers called for the exterminators. Miles out at sea, they cleaned and burned until all the exotic gnats were destroyed. Then they landed in Hawaii, triumphant and pest-free.

No one wants new snakes, biting gnats, or anything else to invade the Hawaiian islands or other environments. But over the years, many animals have been deliberately transported to new places to provide hunting, food, or for other reasons. Now we realize that these animals have changed the ecosystems they have entered. Difficult decisions must be made about the future of exotic species that don't really belong in new environments.

CHAPTER SIX

Mountain Goats— Teetering on the Edge

lympic National Park, in the far northwest corner of Washington state, is a remote area with tall, steep mountains and three saltwater boundaries. Isolated like an island, it has not been an easy place for plants and animals to reach. Ten plant species, five mammal, a salamander, three fish, and numerous butterfly and beetle species live in the Olympic Mountains but exist nowhere else on earth. Grizzly bears, lynx, mountain goats, bighorn sheep, porcupines, bobcats, and other animals live in the Cascade Mountains just seventy-five miles to the east, but they never managed to get established in the Olympics. It is such an unusual area that it has been named a biosphere reserve, and scientists come from all over the world to study it .

THE INVASION
OF THE GOATS

In the 1920s, however, twelve mountain goats were introduced into the Olympic Mountains to provide game for the hunters. The goats

A population of mountain goats
threatens the delicate environment in
Washington's Olympic National Park.

did well on a diet of rare alpine plants, and the population grew to hundreds. The animals liked to climb high into the mountains, often too high for hunters to reach, so the hunters were not a factor in keeping the goat population under control. In 1938, the area was protected as a national park, and hunting was prohibited. The population of goats grew to over twelve hundred animals. Their sharp split hooves, excellent for rock climbing, trampled and destroyed fragile alpine plants. They ate some rare plants and ignored others, causing an imbalance among the plants. As plants disappeared, the food supply for native insects, rodents, deer, and other species was affected.

Dirt baths were another big problem. Goats roll around in the dirt or kick it up onto their backs to get relief from biting insects and the heat. In the process, they dig out huge wallows, some of them thirty feet across. Seventy wallows were found on just one steep meadow, displacing tons of dirt. The disturbed areas cause erosion and open up places where thistle and other invading exotic weeds can take over.

The Olympic Park officials needed to do something to protect this unusual environment. Beginning in the 1970s, they used salt bait and dart guns to capture about four hundred goats. The tranquilized animals were then transported to areas with native goat populations. The remaining goats went higher and higher into the mountains and became increasingly difficult to find. Using a helicopter expert, a park ranger was able to tranquilize and capture a few of these goats—at a cost of $1,000 per animal. In addition to being expensive, this proved hazardous to both people and animals. Some goats slipped and died on the steep slopes after being tranquilized. A survey from July 1997 shows that about three hundred animals remain.

WHAT SHOULD BE DONE
AND WHO DECIDES?

In areas of Olympic National Park where goats have been fenced out or removed, the recovery of native plants has been very strong. Park officials would like to remove all of the goats. After trying ten techniques, they have decided that the safest and most permanent method of doing this would be for park officials to shoot them—at a cost of $40 per goat. This, however, is very controversial and is still being debated. People who would have no trouble removing exotic mosquitoes or snakes have more sympathy for these white woolly creatures. On the other hand, hunters want to keep up the goat population inside the park so they can shoot the ones that stray outside the park boundaries. A native plant society supports complete removal of the exotic invaders, but an animal welfare group wishes to protect the goats in spite of the cost to the ecosystem. Politicians have joined in on the various discussions and evaluations.

A few people suggest that the goats might have been present in the Olympic Park area in the historical past and therefore would not be considered exotic at all. The park consulted nine experts in different fields and all agreed that the goats *are* exotic. No naturalists familiar with the area before 1920 mentioned the goats and no physical evidence of the goats' presence prior to 1920 has been found. Also, historians are sure that "wool dogs" were raised and sheared like sheep by the local tribes. Traditionally, dogs were not kept for this purpose if wool could be gathered from mountain goats nearby.

INVADERS THAT GRAZE

Around the world, the presence of exotic animals like goats continues to affect the environments where they were introduced. A study done on Santa Cruz Island off the coast of California revealed that sheep brought to that island preferred to eat the native plants and ignored the plants that were exotic. Since the island plants never had a need to defend themselves against grazing animals before, they had fewer and shorter spines. The grazing sheep found them easier to eat, and the native plants disappeared. As the ground-nesting birds lost the habitat the plants provided, they died out, too.

A similar problem has occurred on Catalina Island, also off the coast of California. Before refrigeration, ships sailing to remote areas of the world often carried goats along for food. They released goats on islands to go wild and provide them with food in the future. Goats were introduced in this way to Catalina in the 1820s. They began eating native plants like the rare Catalina mahogany, which were reduced to just seven specimens, and ironwood, unable to grow as the goats ate the seedlings. They also removed food and ground cover for the native birds, reptiles, and rodents. In a controversial move meant to restore native species, goats were hunted from helicopters. As the goats disappear, the native plants are sprouting back to life.

Exotic goats are also a huge problem in Australia, as they compete with native animals not only for food, but for water, especially during droughts, and for shelter. Feral goats, the domestic animals gone wild, also carry exotic parasites and diseases like foot rot and foot-and-mouth disease. The rare rock wallaby has been forced out of its rock shelters by wild goats. Without this shelter, the wallaby is easy prey for eagles, foxes, and the extreme heat of the day.

Goats are a problem in the Galapagos Islands off South America as well. This unusual area has nineteen hundred plant and animal species found nowhere else on earth. These include herds of six-hundred-pound tortoises, swimming iguanas that eat sea grass, tropical penguins, and daisies that grow 60 feet tall! There are many problems arising from exotic species on these islands, including those caused by thousands of feral goats, which eat plants that are the natural food source for the rare tortoises. The goats also eat the trees, which provide the unusual water system in this dry area. The trees collect fog, which then drips down as the water source for everything in the ecosystem. When the goats destroy the forest, they destroy the whole community. Thirteen thousand goats were killed in 1996 in an effort to protect these unique islands.

The only place in the world where marine iguanas
can be found is in the waters surrounding the
Galapagos Islands.

Since the Galapagos Islands were only discovered by humans in 1535, they are now in a condition similar to Hawaii's in the 1800s. The problems in Hawaii are now so huge that one Hawaiian scientist referred to exotic goats as "the easy stuff." With knowledge gained through experience and study of the past, people of the 1990s have a better chance of preserving the rare species of the Galapagos. It will take a great effort, however, and the effort may be doomed to failure without the cooperation of the local people. Most of them are very poor fishermen and resent the concern over the native plants and animals. In the 1990s, some of them have shown their frustration by taking hostages at a research station, killing tortoises and threatening to kill Lonesome George, the last surviving tortoise of the Pinta Island species.

Preserving an environment is very difficult, and most people will agree that some degree of change is inevitable. However, it cannot be denied that incredible secrets are locked into everything that we *can* preserve, information that has helped plants and animals to survive for thousands, even millions, of years. Perhaps some of this information will be vital for the survival of our species in a world that now changes so quickly.

CHAPTER SEVEN

From Spiders to Bridges— From Flowers to Medicines

Nature has adapted to all the environments of earth, even the extremes of damp, cold, dark, salty, and blazing hot and dry. Scientists so far have discovered 4,000 different species of mammals, 9,000 species of birds, 19,000 of fishes, and about 250,000 of flowering plants. They have also come across at least 750,000 species of insects, millions of beetle species, and uncountable numbers of species of fungi, worms, algae, and other microorganisms. Each of these species can have millions of different genetic variations. This is the biodiversity of our planet—a planet full of amazing creations able to accomplish wonderful things.

In nature, plants and animals are able to combine a few simple elements like water, carbon, chalk, and sunlight to form complex biological materials. These materials come together without expensive laboratories, assembly lines, or the burning of precious fuels like oil and coal. They start with a few molecules and add more material as needed. In this way, no huge piles of waste are left behind that must be hauled to the dump. If anything is left over, there is always some creature like a dung beetle, a buzzard, or a rodent that will find some use for it.

NATURAL WONDERS

Human inventors would love to discover some of the secrets of nature's creations. Spiders can weave a silk web that is ounce for ounce five times stronger and more elastic than steel. Spiders use flies and crickets as their resource and have been creating this material for over three hundred million years. With a similar material, we might be able to build stronger bridges with a natural ability to rattle and shake during an earthquake without collapsing. Scientists are looking for just the right spider to help them unlock this secret. So far, only one third of some thirty thousand subspecies of spiders have been studied.

The natural world is full of creatures that have made fabulous adaptations to the world around them. Beetles have a hard protective covering called an exoskeleton that springs back into shape after injury. What if we could repair damaged cars like this? Abalone are sea animals also able to heal after an injury. They line their shells with mother-of-pearl, a flashy substance twice as strong as our best ceramics. Slugs produce a slime that protects their soft bodies from punctures. Mussels create a powerful glue that works in cold water, holding them in place even in strong tides. Sharks grow new teeth, frogs revive after being frozen solid, salmon navigate without maps, and some animals hibernate for many months without food. Scientists are eager to understand many of nature's secrets.

CHEMICALLY SPEAKING

Plants and animals have also been concocting chemicals for millions of years, chemicals meant to attract pollinators or to keep predators away.

Although they seem fragile, spider webs are made from a material that is stronger than steel.

Some of these chemicals have been found to affect the human heart, nervous system, muscles, and digestive system. Others reduce inflammation, or fight bacteria, viruses, worms, and cancer.

When scientists discover one of these chemicals, it can have a great impact on human health. For instance, two anticancer drugs have been made from a plant called the rosy periwinkle. The periwinkle was found in Madagascar, a large island in the Indian Ocean where many unique species have already become extinct. Today many children with leukemia are able to survive using the medicine made from periwinkles. Another new life-saving cancer drug is called taxol, discovered in the Pacific yew tree that grows in the last remaining forests of the Pacific Northwest.

One scientist observed that dogfish sharks were often injured in fights with other sharks but didn't suffer any infections from their wounds. After taking a closer look in his laboratory, the scientist discovered a powerful new antibiotic for use in humans. This is especially important today, as some bacteria are not responding to our present supply of antibiotics and new drugs must be developed to fight the threat of infection. Another new medicine, which comes from the venom of the pit viper, helps people to recover from strokes.

STUDYING SAMOA

Scientists are gathering valuable information about unique ecosystems simply by talking with certain people who live there. These people, called traditional healers, know every plant in their surroundings and use roots, leaves, and bark for medicine. In Samoa, for instance, an 82-year-old healer has led scientists to seventy-four different medicinal plants! He has also

Lovely to look at, Madagascar's periwinkles also contain a chemical that has been proven effective in fighting cancer.

provided information about the best season for collecting these plants and what size they should be. Samoa is one of the poorest countries in the world, with a yearly income of only $100 for each person. A foundation has been established to ensure that native Samoans share in any profits from the development of medicines discovered in their environment. Eighty percent of the lowland forests on Samoa are already gone, and the natural ecosystem is at risk. This new source of income creates a potential way to preserve the environment by making money from the forest without destroying it. Programs like this are more likely to succeed when the local people are involved in a positive way.

LOOKING TOWARD
THE FUTURE

Just as we are beginning to study our world with new, high-powered microscopes and other extraordinary tools, pieces of that world are becoming extinct and disappearing every day. Some of this is due directly to the invasion of exotic species, now occurring hundreds of thousands of times faster than the natural process.

As scientists search for additional secrets hidden in the cells of nature, they have a big concern. What happens if the next anticancer plant, the next antibiotic shark, or the spider with the best web becomes extinct before anyone has a chance to study it?

Zoos and seed banks may have programs designed to preserve and protect a few species, but they are unable to protect entire ecosystems. Seed banks, for instance, where seeds are selected and preserved at very cold temperatures, cannot possibly hold all the genetic diversity that would exist in the wild. How would a plant fare if it disappeared from the wild and was then reintroduced from a seed bank? It would only survive if the pollinator, the root fungi, and all other necessary interdependent pieces of its environment were still available.

Seed banks can only hope to save a fragment of earth's diverse plant population.

The best way to preserve the earth's biodiversity is to maintain natural ecosystems and let nature do the work of keeping things in balance. But that is not always possible. As nature becomes overwhelmed with too many exotic species, there are many things people can do to help. In Oregon, each mile of beach is assigned a volunteer who patrols the shore, looking for an exotic grass called spartina, which is changing the beach environment. Unlike the native sea grass, spartina traps sediment and raises the height of the mudflat. This eliminates places where oysters can burrow and where some salmon like to eat. Every time the grass moves into his or her territory, the volunteer yanks it out.

In Hawaii, high school students called "Weed Warriors" spend Saturdays on patrol, searching for and destroying alien plants. A Hawaiian newspaper carries an ad for the "10 Most Unwanted" plants, and people call a hot line when they spot one of them.

Hot lines also exist in the Great Lakes region, part of the fight against invading zebra mussels.

As people become more aware of the threat of exotic species, they are often willing to make sure they are not transporting any when they travel, even if it means throwing away a bag of fruit or a potted plant.

Scientists now screen biological controls very carefully to ensure that one pest does not replace another. In the last twenty years, more than 90 percent of the introduced biological controls have been successful, but they are few and far between. New studies are also focusing on native pollinators, in serious decline because much of their food—the native plants—have been replaced by farm crops and cities or killed by pesticides and exotic species. Honeybees are not native pollinators. They are exotic species brought to the United States from Europe for their honey. They are often raised in hives and delivered to farm fields to pollinate crops at a time when they will not be affected by chemical sprays. Exotic honeybees have been encouraged at the expense of at least four thousand species of native bees, although native bees are able to do a better job of pollination. Four native mason bees can pollinate an apple tree in the time it takes hundreds of honeybees to do the job.

In the last few years, over half the honeybees have been killed by new exotic species—mites and an aggressive invading African bee. This is a serious problem, because many plants and farm crops depend on honeybees for pollination, and many creatures then depend on these crops and plants for food. With the decline of honeybees, people are attempting to increase the populations of native pollinators by making new homes for native bees. They drill 3/16-inch holes about 5 inches deep into wood and sometimes line these nesting holes with drinking straws for easier cleaning after the bees emerge. Others are growing native plants to attract local bees, butterflies, and hummingbirds. Some groups are working with highway departments to establish native plants on median strips along the road. In Texas, for instance, bluebonnets and Indian paintbrush now line the roads. Even a small window box garden can help provide food for the native pollinators. Larger populations of native pollinators will reduce our dependence on exotic pollinators and at the same time prevent the loss of native plants.

The importance of realizing that plants, animals, and people are connected in a delicate balance, and how easily that balance can be threatened, cannot be ignored. Unique communities like islands, forests, prairies, and deserts can hardly exist today without our care and attention. The loss of these natural ecosystems diminishes human existence in ways we are just beginning to understand. Each unique environment is a treasure, and every loss makes us poorer.

Glossary

Biodiversity—The variety of living things, numbering in the millions, that thrive in different environments all over the world. "Bio" means life, "diversity" means differences.

Biological Control—A natural enemy of an exotic species, such as a predator, parasite, or disease, that can keep it under control.

Biosphere Reserve—A system set up by the United Nations to preserve selected unique areas of the world for research, education, and protection of their diversity.

Byssus—Clumps of threads secreted by zebra mussels that allow them to stick to hard surfaces like rocks, pipes, boats, and logs.

Ecosystem—A community of plants, animals, and bacteria and the water, climate, and soil around it.

Endangered—A species that once thrived on earth but now exists in such low numbers that most of its diversity is gone and it may soon become extinct.

Extinct—A species once living on earth but now lost forever.

Feral—Domestic, tame animals that have become wild, like pigs, goats, cats, or dogs let loose, or cultivated plants that have become wild.

Herbicide—A chemical used to destroy unwanted plants or to slow down their growth.

Node—The joint on a plant stem where a leaf starts to grow.

Plankton—Microscopic plant (phytoplankton) and animal (zooplankton) life found floating in water and important as a food source for fish and mussels.

Pollinator—An insect, bird, or other creature that carries plant pollen to allow the plant to reproduce. With very light pollen, the pollinator can be the wind.

Predator—A creature that goes after another creature for its food.

Veliger—The microscopic larvae stage of a zebra mussel that is carried by currents before the larvae settle and form shells.

Further Reading

Collard, Sneed B. III. *Alien Invaders: The Continuing Threat of Exotic Species.* Danbury, CT: Franklin Watts, 1996.

Guiberson, Brenda Z. *Spotted Owl: Bird of the Ancient Forest.* New York: Henry Holt, 1994.

Lesinski, Jeanne M. *Exotic Invaders: Killer Bees, Fire Ants, and Other Alien Species Are Invading America!* New York: Walker, 1996.

Patent, Dorothy Hinshaw. *Back to the Wild.* San Diego: Harcourt Brace, 1997.

———. *Biodiversity.* New York: Clarion, 1996.

Pringle, Laurence. *Living Treasure: Saving Earth's Threatened Biodiversity.* New York: Morrow Junior Books, 1991.

Seibert, Patricia. *Toad Overload: A True Tale of Nature Knocked Off Balance in Australia.* Brookfield, CT: Millbrook Press, 1996.

Silverstein, Alvin, Virginia Silverstein, and Laura Silverstein Nunn. *The Black-Footed Ferret.* Brookfield, CT: Millbrook Press, 1995.

flickers, 21
flying squirrels, 10
foxes, 10
frogs, 9, 13, 68
fruit flies, 15
fungus, 10

Galapagos Islands, 64, *65*, 66
glochidia, 35
goats, 60, *61*, 62-64
grasshoppers, 24
Great Lakes, 38-40, 45, 74
Guam, 55-56
Guam flycatchers, 56

Haleakala National Park, 53
Hawaiian Islands, 46-56, 59, 66, 74
hawks, 9, 10
herbicides, 29
hibernation, 68
honeybees, 74
honeycreepers, 10, 47, 53, 55
honeydew, 12
Hudson River, 39

iguanas, 64, *65*
Illinois River, 39
Indian paintbrush, 75
ironwood, 65

Japanese white eyes, 55

kudzu, 24, 25-26, *27*, 28-29, *29*, *30*, 31-32, *33*, 34, 51

Lacy Act of 1900, 24
Lake Erie, 38-40
Lake St. Clair, 35, 37

Laysan Island, 53
Laysan rails, 53
lobelia, 53
Lonesome George, 66

Madagascar, 70
mamo birds, 48
marine iguanas, 64, *65*
medicine, 31-32, 70, *71*, 72
Micronesia, 59
Mississippi River, 39
mongooses, 49, *49*
mosquitoes, 50-51
moths, 10, *12*
mountain goats, 60*, 61,* 62-63
muskrats, 15-16, *16*
mussels, 68
    native, 39-40, 42, 45
    zebra, 35, *36*, 37-42, *38*, *41*, *43*, 44-45, 74

National Aeronautics and Space Administration (NASA), 45
native mussels, 39-40, 42, 45
nenes (Hawaiian goose), 49, *50*
Netherlands, 15-16, 24, 42
night hawk moths, 10, *12*

ohia trees, 48
Ohio River, 39
Olympic National Park, 60, *61*, 62-63
orange-foot pimpleback mussels, 45
Oregon beaches, 73
Oriental bittersweet, 34
owls, 9, 10
oxpecker birds, 12-13
oysters, 73